This is

MY UNTOLD STORY.

©The Life Graduate Publishing Group

No part of this book may be scanned, reproduced or distributed in any printed or electronic form without the prior permission of the author or publisher.

ABOUT THE AUTHOR

Name:

Signature

"Mother is the name for God in the lips and hearts of little children."
— William Makepeace Thackeray

The Beginning.....

Full Name at Birth

Date of Birth   /   /

Time of Birth   :

Day of the week you were born?

Height at birth?

Weight at birth?

Place of Birth (include the City/Town, Country)

Did you have any siblings when you were born? If so, what were their names and their ages?

Add any additional notes or information here...

The Beginning.....

Share with us some information about your parents?

____

____

____

____

What have you been told about you as a baby?

____

____

Did you have any unique characteristics or funny things you did as a baby?

____

____

____

Add any additional notes or information here...

The Beginning.....

What were your first words?

____

Were you in good health as a baby?

____

____

Do you have any other baby memories to share?

____

____

____

____

____

____

"The influence of a mother in the lives of her children is beyond calculation."
—James E. Faust

Childhood Years

What was your favorite toy growing up?

Did you have a pet or any pets growing up?

What was your favorite T.V show to watch as a child?

Was there a moment you remember getting into big trouble as a child? Was there a punishment?

Add any additional notes or information here...

Childhood Years

What are your fondest memories growing up between the ages of 5 years to 12 years?

Add any additional notes or information here...

Childhood Years

Where did you grow up as a child?
(house,location, town etc)

____

____

____

____

Who was your best friend or your best friends as a child?

____

____

What was your favorite day of the week and why?

____

____

____

____

"There is no role in life that is more essential than that of motherhood."
—Elder M. Russell Ballard

Childhood Years

What was your favorite meal as a child?

____

What elementary/primary school did you attend and where was it located?

____

____

Describe your most memorable moment or story from elementary/primary school.

____

____

____

____

____

____

____

____

Add any additional notes or
information here...

Teenage Years..

Describe your dress sense and clothing as a teenager. Is there anything that stands out for you?

When and where did you learn to drive a vehicle?

What was your first vehicle and how much did you purchase it for? Tell us your special 'first car' story!

Add any additional notes or information here...

Teenage Years..

What High School did you attend and where was it located?

____

____

____

Who was you favorite teacher or coach and why?

____

____

____

What was your favorite subject at school?

____

____

____

Did you date anyone at High School?

____

____

____

"There is no influence so powerful
as that of the mother."
—Sara Josepha Hale

Teenage Years..

What hobbies did you have as a teenager?

What is your most memorable moment as a teenager?

If you knew what you know today, what would you have done differently as a teenager?

Add any additional notes or information here...

Did you have a close friendship group? Have you maintained contact with any of them?

____

____

____

____

Did you have any nicknames at High School?

____

____

What 5 words come to mind to describe your teenage years?

1. ____

2. ____

3. ____

4. ____

5. ____

When I was a child, my mode of transport to school was..

____

____

When I was in my teens, the biggest news story that I recall was .....

____

____

____

When I was growing up, my 3 favorite movies were:

1. ____

2. ____

3. ____

"A mother's arms are more comforting than anyone else's."
— Princess Diana

Add any additional notes or
information here...

When I was .....

When I was a child, the first movie I went to the theatre to see was..

When I graduated from elementary/primary school, the year was..

When I was 8 years old, I wanted to be a......

When I was 18 years old, my favorite music and band was..

When I was in my teens, the most popular thing to do on a Saturday night was.......

When I was young, I loved to travel to.......

This is my Untold Story...

Family History

My grandparents names were:

Grandmother: _______________________

Grandfather: _______________________

They were born in: (country)
Grandmother: _______________________

Grandfather: _______________________

This is something that not many people may know about
our family history……

____

____

____

____

Additional Family History information:

____

____

____

Our FAMILY TREE

Grandfather

Grandfather

Grandmother

Grandmother

Mother

Father

Me

Add any additional notes or information here...

Parenthood

How old were you when you first became a parent?

____

Explain how you felt emotionally when you bacame a parent for the first time?

____

____

____

____

____

Where were you located (city/town/country) when you had your first child?

____

____

____

Add any additional notes or
information here...

Parenthood

What has been the biggest challenge for you as a parent?

____

____

____

____

What are 3 key responsibilities you believe are important as a parent?

1 ____

____

2 ____

____

3 ____

____

"A mother's happiness is like a beacon, lighting up the future but reflected also on the past in the guise of fond memories."
— Honore de Balzac

Parenthood

Expand on any further parenting memories you may like to share

"A mother's love is more beautiful
than any fresh flower."
— Debasish Mridha

This is my Untold Story...

More about me!

Not many people know this about me, so let me share it with you:

____

____

____

____

____

____

The activity or hobby that I enjoy most to do now is.....

____

____

I have the unique ability to be able to....

____

____

____

Add any additional notes or information here...

More about me!

If I was able to go back to a special time in history, it would be...

If I could pass on one word of advice to others, it would be..

There are special moments in life that you wish you could pause to enjoy for longer. Mine would be......

"A mother's love is everything. It is what brings a child into this world. It is what molds their entire being. When a mother sees her child in danger, she is literally capable of anything. Mothers have lifted cars off of their children and destroyed entire dynasties. A mother's love is the strongest energy known to man."
—Jamie McGuire

This is my Untold Story...

More about me!

I wish I had the opportunity to...

____

____

____

The quote that resonates most with me is..

____

____

____

____

My favorite book of all time is:

____

If there is one thing I would like to be remembered for it would be:

____

____

____

Add any additional notes or information here...

More about me!

When I look back on my life so far, my 3 proudest moments are:

1

2

3

If there were 3 famous people that I could invite for dinner they would be:

1

2

3

This is my Untold Story...

Add any additional notes or
information here...

More about me!

From my teen years, these are the jobs that I've had:

____

____

____

____

____

____

____

____

____

"When you look at your mother, you are looking at the purest love you will ever know."
— Mitch Albom

More about me!

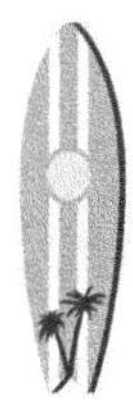

One of the jobs that stands out as my most enjoyable has been..

____

____

The most interesting place I have ever traveled to has been.... (include the year/date this occurred)

____

____

____

If I was given a free return flight to anywhere in the world, I would visit...(include your 'Why')

____

____

____

____

This is my Untold Story...

Final Notes...

There have been many questions that I have answered in
this book, but I would also like to share this with you...

*Your time to write anything else you
wish to share*

Final Notes...

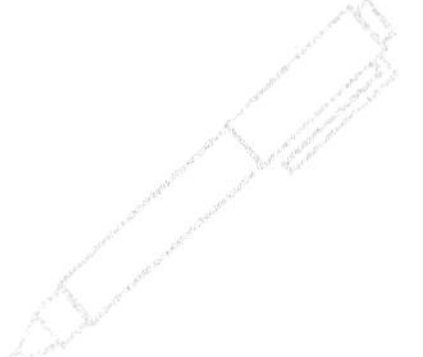

Your time to write anything else you wish to share

"If love is as sweet as a flower,
then my mother is that sweet flower
of love."
—Stevie Wonder

Memories

Memories

Memories

Memories

This is my Untold Story

www.ingramcontent.com/pod-product-compliance
Lightning Source LLC
Chambersburg PA
CBHW080503030726
47592CB00011B/3230